Yes, seniors can click with computers and the Internet, 1 byte at a time.
Yes, seniors can click with computers and the Internet, 1 byte at a time.
Yes, seniors can click with computers and the Internet, 1 byte at a time.

Name_____

CLASS EMAIL
ADDRESS_____

PASSWORD_____

Seniors, Want or Need

Basic Computer Skills?

A DR. KATIE CANTY COMPUTER ACADEMY BASICS BOOK

No Prior Computer Experience Necessary

Very easy, fun, friendly learning activities

Yes, seniors can click with computers and the Internet, 1 byte at a time

Yes, seniors can click with computers and the Internet, 1 byte at a time.

Yes, seniors can click with computers and the Internet—1 byte at a time.

Welcome Senior Technology Computer Academy Participant
Fill This in First

My full name is _____

Start date_____

Completion date_____

Name of professor <u>Dr. Katie Canty</u>   <u>seniortechacademy@yahoo.com</u>

Senior center location _____

My email address is _____

My password_____

Each student has a new class email address. Check inside your course folder.

Your goal(s)

What do you plan to use your computer skills for upon completion of this course?

_____

Your question(s)

Do you have a special question about computers, this class, or a suggestion? If so, write it here.

_____

COMPUTER TECHNOLOGY WORKSHOPS
WORKSHOP 1 COMPUTER WORDS/TERMS
Word Meanings--What To Press, Touch, Mash
To Get Started?

1. Understand the use of some basic computer terms.
2. Begin a very short online computer keyboarding course.

WORKSHOP 2 INTERNET
How to Go To Internet Websites

1. Go to websites for news, weather, sports, or entertainment.
2. Explore some currently cool and useful websites.
3. Google or Wikipedia research a topic(s).

WORKSHOP 3 E-MAIL
How to Compose, Send, & Open Your Email Messages

1. Log into your email account.
2. Compose and send an email.
3. Open and read email with attachments.
4. Save to a USB removable drive.

WORKSHOP 4 SOCIAL NETWORKS
How to Social Network Online with Family & Friends

1. Post messages and pictures to a Facebook account.
2. Find family and friends to chat with.

WORKSHOP 5 ONLINE SELLING
How to Get Started Selling Your Crafts Online—eBay & Etsy

1. Register for 2 accounts, eBay account plus Paypal account.
2. Take photos, list it, ship it, and get paid.

WORKSHOP 6   WORD PROCESSING
How to Prepare and Print Cards, Event Documents, Articles
1. Take and upload photos to a document(s).
2. Open, create, save, edit, print, return to tweak as required.

WORKSHOP 7   POWERPOINT
How to Prepare & Present Your Photo-Essay Memoirs
1. Create a personal photo story presentation.
2. Prepare a speech on a topic of interest to you.

WORKSHOP 8 BOOKS: CREATE & PUBLISH YOURS
How Not To Go Broke Creating & Publishing Your Book(s)
1. Create and publish a hard copy book or an electronic eBook.
2. Use Createaspace self-publishing website—free of charge.

WORKSHOP 9 HANDHELD COMPUTER DEVICES
How to Use More of the Features of an Ipad & Smartphone
1. Explore the latest and greatest features of hand held devices.
2. Take online virtual and real time hand held device field trips.
3. Discover new computer applications that enrich the lives of seniors.
4. BYOD, bring your own device and send spectacular photos.

INTRODUCTION
The Academy for Senior Technology Program

Some of you might have participated in or read about Senior Computer Technology Academy celebrations. The graduation celebrations are beautiful. Here is a synopsis from *The Wilmington Journal* articles.

The senior students dressed in the same color—white for women and black or navy for men. A wonderful speaker praised their efforts to the applause of a joyful audience filled with relatives and friends. The oldest graduate was 89.

One highly dedicated student was selected as the valedictorian and received the prestigious Mouse Pad Honor Award. A reception followed the awarding of certificates.

Dr. Canty, who collaborates with senior centers, colleges and universities to spread senior citizen computer literacy everywhere, noticed that quite a few students were either retired military citizens, or spouses of retired military who had chosen to spend their "golden computer literate years" in the local region. The students enrolled in a morning or an afternoon class. The classes were offered at multiple campus locations, including a location in a low-income housing project's education center.

Each academy has a different celebration theme. One celebration was hosted to applaud the efforts of retired military veterans, spouses of military veterans, and civilian technology boot camp participants who are victoriously bridging the local digital divide—one byte at a time.

Mission Statement

The mission and vision of this computer technology academy is development and demonstration of basic, intermediate, or advance computer literacy skills by 100% of course completers.

DEDICATION

To Jaimee who supports and attends every
senior technology academy event

To facility directors, class participants,
and eighty plus year old honor graduates

CONTENTS

Fill-in Form

Welcome 9:30-11:30AM Computer Academy Participants
MISSION/VISION: COMPUTER TECHNOLOGY LITERACY, 1 BYTE AT A TIME
SYLLABUS

WORKSHOP DATES:
TEXT: *Seniors, Want or Need Basic Computer Skills?* by Dr. Katie Canty available at amazon.com or from the instructor
PROFESSOR: Dr. Katie Canty

GOAL: One hundred per cent of course completers should demonstrate an ability to digitally communicate using basic computer literacy skills

INSTRUCTIONAL METHODS: Discussion, question and answer, online research, hands-on computer practice, student and team presentations, final individual or class project
Note: If needed or wanted, a computer and help are available in county libraries and community college libraries that have computers for public use.

COMMUNICATION
• Email message to: seniortechacademy@yahoo.com
• Call the center director: Leave a clear message with a call-back number.

CLASS PROCEDURES
• Cell phones on silence or vibrate before class begins
• Food/beverage consumption allowed in designated area(s)—not on or near computer work stations
• Restroom facilities used on an as-needed basis

15 minutes
1. Review and/or completion of past week's workshop(s)
35 minutes
2. Introduction and discussion of current week's new material
10 minutes ------ BREAK TIME
35 minutes
3. Individual student lab work completion
5 minutes
4. Preview of upcoming week's topics and computer labs

PERFORMANCE OBJECTIVES AND EXPECTATIONS

In addition to demonstration of attentiveness, thoughtfulness, and respect, there are six things that each participant is expected to demonstrate upon completion of workshop activities:

1. turn a computer on and off
2. create and print a usable, effective document
3. create, send, and open email
4. use the Internet to get information from a website
5. safely use computers for networking, fun, work, or resource management
6. begin a useful computer project related to a training lesson(s)

COURSE DESCRIPTION CLASS HOURS

　8 hours　Senior Center Workshops with Professor Canty
　4 hours　Computer Lab Practice at Senior Center, Library, or Home

PREREQUISITES: NONE

USB FLASH/JUMP DRIVE (OPTIONAL PURCHASE)

ATTENDANCE

 Attend at least 3 of 4 classes--1 time a week for 2 hours

GRADES

A course completion certificate document will be issued to course completers, preferably during the academy graduation celebration.

ACADEMY CELEBRATION CEREMONY – CERTIFICATE

For course completers in attendance at the senior technology academy celebration ceremony, an instructor's certificate of participation will be presented to each student during the ceremony. A prestigious, valedictorian-like MOUSE PAD HONOR AWARD will be presented to a selected student(s).

Ceremony participation is highly encouraged, however, participation is optional. Information will be given to students in time for invitations to be sent to family, friends, co-workers, club members, etc.

WORKSHOP 1
BASIC COMPUTER WORDS/TERMS

USUALLY ANSWERS QUESTIONS SUCH AS
What button do I mash to get this computer do what I want?

WORKSHOP 1

UNDERSTAND SOME
BASIC COMPUTER TERMINOLOGY

In this workshop, let's learn along with Kenney and Barbee about some basic **computer** components and terminology. Let's get started.

Kenny and Barbee kept asking everybody they saw that day for help with the new computer. The children, grandchildren, great grandbaby and even the puppy were asked to help Kenny and Barbee to understand how to use the computer.

For a gift, the children bought Kenney and Barbee a new, up-to-date computer with a large screen designed especially for seniors. The new computer has all kinds of **hardware** like a **mouse** and a **removable disk drive** plus **software** like **Word** and **PowerPoint**. Their children know how important it is to work on the best, up-to-date, working computer that has a good, reliable **Internet service provider**. Kenny and Barbee's **standalone computer**, **mobile hand held devices,** and **Internet** service are provided by a telephone company.

WORKSHOP 1
Let's Get Comfortable With Operating A Computer

Let's participate in the senior center day one of computer class along with your classmates, Kenneth and Barbara McCyber. Let's get started with the first basic—turning on, **logging in**, opening a screen, exiting, and turning off a **personal computer (PC)**.

1. BEGIN ORIENTATION—First, use a pencil or pen to fill in the *Getting Started Complete This First* Sheet in the front of the book. Read the course introduction and syllabus. For now, just scan the rest of the book to get an idea of what we will study as the course moves forward.

2. TURN THE COMPUTER ON – If you hear the phrase "boot up," that means to turn the computer on. The computer is usually turned on by pushing a button, touching the screen, or issuing a voice command. Most computers will emit some color of light during this stage, and the color of the screen will usually change from black/gray to blue.

3. LOG IN – This usually involves **keying/typing** in a **user name** or a **password** and sometimes both a user name and or password. For example, at the local library the user name is the long number on the back of the library card. The password is the last four digits of this long number.

The words "typing" and "keying" mean just about the same thing. Keying refers to pressing the keys on the computer keyboard to get alphabets, numbers, and symbols to appear on the **monitor screen**. The monitor or screen looks like a television screen that shows what one is keying, and it also shows videos, pictures, movies, or images to look at.

Find out what user name or password is required to log on to the computer, and key it in.

4. LOG ONTO THE INTERNET—this usually means locating the E on the opening screen and clicking on it. If there is no big E, look down to the right bottom of the screen and click on the start button. When a dialogue box appears, click on **Internet**. The Internet is a lot of connected telephones and satellites that talk to each other globally and perhaps inter-planetary.

5. OPEN UP A SOFTWARE DOCUMENT SCREEN TO TYPE/KEY
Today's computer's come with some kind of basic software for keying stuff. **Software** is a computer package or program designed to tell a computer what to do. Software can be anything from basic games to complex business systems software. Log in and open up a word processing program screen. Click on start programs and look for Word, Works, or Note Pad—these are popular word processing programs that usually come all ready loaded on a computer.

6. SAVE AS – If something is typed that needs to be used again, then the information needs to be saved to a **removable flash drive**, stored on your **PC--personal computer**'s **hard drive,** or to **the cloud**—not the business, library, or someone else's computer; otherwise, when the computer is turned off, the information is gone and has to be re-entered. A few students have been known to work on a document for a long time, then just close and shut down the computer without saving. This meant that all the long hours of work was lost because the information keyed in was not saved. When we get to the word processing training, saving and something called "save as" will be a part of the training.

7. END ORIENTATION: TURN OFF A COMPUTER—To get a computer to shut down and turn itself off, do this. Look towards the bottom left of the screen for a start **button.** A button is like a little square shape tab with something written on it. Get hold of the mouse, and move it downward the word start--a **large I** will appear and turn into an arrow. Point the **arrow** to start and press down on the right side of the mouse—this is a **right click**. A dialogue box is going to appear. Click on log off or it the shut down wording.

Answer the Workshop 1 Show & Tell Questions.
COMPUTER TERMINOLOGY
FILL-IN QUESTIONS

Do you understand the words coming off this page? Time to THINK, read, re-read, write down, and discuss. **Write down or draw a description** of each of the following terms as we discuss the terms.

1. **Computer** _____

2. **Internet provider** _____

3. **Handheld Device(s)**_____

4. **Monitor/Screen**_____

5. **CPU** _____

6. **Hardware** _____

7. **Software** _____

8. **Mouse**_____

9. **Internet** _____

10.   **Toggles** _____

11.   **Swipe** _____

12.   **Apps** _____

13.   **Cloud** _____

14.   **Scan** _____

15.   **Blog** _____

16.   **Viral** _____

17.   **Website** _____

WORKSHOP 1
CONTROL YOUR MOUSE

Let's find out how to use computer **hardware** and **software** along with Kenney and Barbee. What do you mean by "**click on**," asks Kenney? Dr. Byte goes to his desk and shows him **the mouse**.

The mouse is a point to something device that has two compartments separated by a round cylinder in the middle. When I say "click on" that means to gently grab hold to the mouse like this: place the thumb on the right side and the 4th and 5th fingers on the other side. Hover your second and third fingers over the right compartment and press down to click.

COMPLETE THIS MOUSE CONTROL COMPUTER PRACTICE

Practice controlling the mouse. Do these 4 things:

1. scroll (Note the triangles and the cylinder in the middle of the mouse.)

2. right click (Thumb on one side of mouse, last two fingers on other side: Press down with the third finger on the right side of the mouse.)

3. double click (Press down two times.)

4. select (Key your first name, then select it by clicking the mouse. Hold the mouse and move it horizontally across your name until shading appears. If correctly selected, the name will be a shaded color.)

WORKSHOP 1
CONTROL YOUR I-BEAM AND ARROW

"What about this here blinking little straight line that looks like an I, what's that doing there, asked Barbee?"

Dr. Byte said, "**key** the word computer on your screen. Now, if you want to click on the word computer, do this. Hold the mouse, and move it upward. Do you see an "I" as you began to move the mouse? This is an **I-Beam** that lets you **click** in front the word or letter that you want. Place the I Beam in front of the "c" in computer and it will turn back to the I and start blinking—the **insertion point**. The blinking light lets you know that you can start typing from this point. **The I-Beam is like a placeholder or beacon that lets you know where you are in a document.**

"What about this here arrow, asks Kenney?" When I move the mouse upward towards the top of the screen where you say I can find something called **menus**, I notice that **an arrow** comes up. What's that there arrow for?"

The arrows are for scrolling and issuing commands to the computer. Move the mouse forward towards the printer **icon**—an icon is a picture. Wait a few seconds and a message will appear indicating that when you click, the computer will receive **a command** to open the printer **dialogue box** for you so that you can print something.

Complete Workshop 1 Hands-on Computer Practice.
I-BEAM and INSERTION POINT INDICATOR

1. Move the mouse towards the top of the screen. Hold the arrow over the first 4 icons. What commands can you issue for each icon?

2. Move the mouse towards the **Word File** and then click.

3. Save the document with your name and the word computer on it as Chapter 4. To do this click on **Save As**, then select **Desktop** when asked where to save it. Type in the name ch4. (Do not type the punctuation period, just ch4).

4. Click on **Save**.

5. Look on the desktop. Do you see the document name? Ask for help, if you need to.

6. Open the document.

7. Click on **File** again.

8. Assume that you have finished for the day, click on exit under the File tab.

9. Shut down and turn off the computer.

10. Wait a few minutes.

11. Turn the computer back on.

12. Go to **Word** on the desktop. Click.

13. When it opens, click on File and **Open**.

14. Locate the ch4 document and click Open**.**

15. Key "I am doing great.**"**

Complete Workshop 1 Hands-on Computer Practice.

Do you understand the words coming off this page? Time to THINK about it. Learn how to apply each of these terms by showing the instructor, librarian, or tutor how to apply the term; or in your own words, write a definition.

1. **Save/Save As** _____

2. **Commands** _____

3. **Menu** _____

4. **Maximize/Minimize**_____

5. **Desktop**_____

6. **Click on** _____

7. **Boot** _____

8. **Log In/Log out**_____

9. **Icon** _____

10. **Scroll** _____

11. **Text**_____

12. **IM/Instagram**_____

Complete Workshop 1 Self–Test by circling the correct words in each question.

1. Three examples of **computer hardware** are:
a.   This book
b.   A printer
c.   A flash drive also known as an USB or jump drive
d.   Word
e.   PowerPoint
f.   _____my understanding of the meaning

2. Three examples of computer software are:
a.   This book
b.   A keyboard
c.   A QuickBooks program CD
d.   A computer desk and chair
e.   Microsoft Office
_____my understanding of the meaning

3. An **Internet Service Provider (ISP)** is
a.   The company that provides you with Internet service
b.   The place where one buys a computer
c.   Bill Gates
d.   A smart phone
e.   The people who manufacture computers
f.   _____my understanding of the meaning

4. A computer is a
a.   a machine that is smarter than people
b.   an electronic being capable of helping us to think better
c.   a machine that can be programmed to work with other machines
d.   all of the above
e.   none of the above
f. _____my understanding of meaning

WORKSHOP 1
ONLINE KEYBOARD SHORT COURSE
Let's Get Comfortable Using the Computer Key Board

To access your online course go to **www.goodtyping.com**. Key in your class **email address** and **password**. If your are not in a class, complete the registration information for access. The website allows you to practice using both hands and all your fingers to make capital letters, to space between words, to type text, numbers and symbols. Can you complete **9 of the very short lessons in 4 weeks ? Strive to complete 9 or more lessons.**

Hands-on Computer Practice in an Online Course

1. With the Internet up, scroll to and click in the URL box.

2. Key this in the URL box: **www.goodtyping.com**

3. Practice and finish keying lesson 1. It takes about 5 to 10 minutes for a beginner to key a lesson. **Important**: The Caps lock key is a **toggle key** like a light switch—meaning that pressing it turns it on, and pressing it again turns it off. The Caps lock key is sometimes pressed accidently, and it will lock up the good typing lesson. Press the Caps Lock key again to unlock it so that it will move again.

What is your number of words keyed per minute in Lesson 1? _____

How many errors?_____

WORKSHOP 2
THE INTERNET

USUALLY ANSWERS QUESTIONS SUCH AS
COMPUTERS & ME: HOW DO YOU GET THE RIGHT ONE TO WOR?

WORKSHOP 2
THE INTERNET
How to Google & Internet Research A Topic

Step 1: Look towards the top of the screen. Locate the URL white box. With the mouse, point to this box and click in it.

Step 2: Press delete or backspace to get rid of any words in the box.

Step 3: Key/type the topic words you are researching in the URL box or the Google box: the words are in the black bold letters in your question.

Step 4: Press Enter after typing the key research words.

Many titles usually will show up pertaining to the subject. Click on and read through a few to see which one provides the kind of answer that you are looking for.

Let's select, open, view, and discuss a few of these cool and useful websites.

1. wikipedia	7. online bank
2. state treasury	8. 123greetings
3. aarp	9. rxlist
4. sundaycoupons	10. news
5. weather	11. sports
6. youtube	12. overstock

Complete the Workshop 2 Hands-on Computer Practice.
Select and complete any 3 of 5.

SEARCH FOR ONLINE INFORMATION
Get online maps, addresses, people info, facts, and directions

1st Internet Research Practice

goggle.com
GOOGLE YOURSELF BY KEYING YOUR FIRST AND LAST NAME
To find out information about people like yourself, use GOOGLE like this:

1. With the Internet up type goggle.com in the URL box. Press the Enter key and wait a few seconds.

2. When the GOGGLE box appears, Google your name: **key your first name, the plus symbol, and key your last name**. Here's an example: Jane+Doe

3. Press the Enter key after keying your name with the plus symbol.

4. Click on some of the results showing.

2nd Internet Research Practice

whitepages.com
FIND YOUR ADDRESS ON WHITE PAGES
To find a mailing address or telephone number, use white pages like this:

1. Click on the Internet to open it--do this on most computers by clicking on the big E.

2. Look at the top of the screen to find the URL box. This is usually where you will see an e and a large white space with another URL address all ready in it.

3. Delete or backspace to erase what is in the white box at the top of the screen.

4. Key in whitepages.com (no spaces).

5. Press enter.

 To Google a person, subject, news, topic
Repeat steps 1 and 2 above.

- After deleting or backspacing over what is in the URL box at the top of the screen, key in any subject, name, or group of words.

- Important: space between words when goggling

3rd Internet Research Practice
webmd.com
GET AND STAY HEALTHIER
1. Open the Internet and key in the **URL box** webmd.com—avoid making typos.

2. Click in the box just below the date.

3. Type in the word apples or apple cider vinegar.

4. Read the article on apple cider vinegar.

5. What's something new that you learned about apples_____

6. Type in the name of a medicine or condition that you may want to learn more about.

4th Internet Research Lab
mapquest.com
GET STEP-BY-STEP TO & FROM DIRECTIONS USING MAP QUEST
According to MapQuest, how many states would be crossed while driving from your home ZIP code to a Rodeo Drive, Hollywood, CA ZIP code? _____
To answer the above question and to get step-by-step directions, do this:
1. With the Internet up, key map quest in the URL box.

2. Press enter after keying.

3. Click on Directions and wait.

4. When the site comes up, key in your street address.

5. Click in the Zip code box and type your 5 digit ZIP.

6. Next go over to the End area and click in the Street address box. Type in Rodeo Drive.

7. Click in the City box and type the word Hollywood.

8. Click in the State box and type the initials CA.

9. Click on GET DIRECTIONS.

5th Internet Research Lab
CONDUCT CRITICAL THINKING ONLINE RESEARCH
FIND MULTI-SOURCE FACTS AND ANSWERS
1. What are the top three most useful technology gadgets this year?

2. What is the secret to happiness?

WORKSHOP 3   EMAIL

USUALLY ANSWERS QUESTIONS SUCH AS
Did you check your email? I sent you an invitation.

WORKSHOP 3
E-MAIL BASICS
Snail Mail or Email It?

My son keeps talking about how he sent me some kind of new **virtual** gift. I've been checking our mail for 2 weeks now and not a thing was there from that boy. "It's a gift he sent **online** and it's probably in our new **email** box, says Barbee."

HOW IT WORKS – EMAIL ORIENTATION
At senior tech academy, learning to use email is easy, but it takes practice. Here's an easy to use email terminology list and overview.

1. **URL box**—Click on the Internet button to open it. The URL box is the long box at the very top of the screen that comes up after clicking on the big e to that opens up the Internet.

2. **URL website address**-The URL address is a cyber space name for a person, place, business, or thing located online. The **URL address has a dot/period in it**—like yahoo.com. Make the dot with the period symbol.

3. **Email address** – This is like your home address. It's just located in cyber space where satellites and telephone lines bring non-paper, soft copy mail instead of a postal employee bringing hard copy mail. **Email addresses always have the @ symbol**. To make the @ symbol hold down the shift key and keep it down while typing the number 2.

4. **User Name**—This is like your unique telephone number that is different from everyone else's. **A user name has to be different from others**. Yes, a person's name can be used for a user name; however, if someone else has the same name, then numbers or letters have to be added to make the name unique. For example, Kenney wanted the user name, kmccyber@yahoo.com, but the system showed that someone else had this name; therefore, Kenney added 007 to make his user name unique like kmccyber007@yahoo.com.

5. **Password**— This is like your house key and other keys that grant access to stuff. No one else should be able to access or to read your email without your password.

6. **Inbox** - This is where your new email arrives and where you keep your email until you delete it. Once you open an email you get 3 choices - do you want to reply, forward, or delete it?

7. **Write or Compose email** – This is a special place for creating a new email. The CC means that you can send someone else, or a group of people, a copy of the same message. Click on New in Yahoo to compose new mail.

8. **Address Book** - The address book is where you keep track of the email addresses for your friends and family.

9. **Mail Sent** - A copy of the email you've sent is kept in case you need to use it again later.

10. **Trash** - Deleted emails are kept here until you want to get rid of them.

11. **Viruses and Spam** – Viruses will keep a computer from working properly and spam is usually a lot of unwanted advertisements and solicitations.

WORKSHOP 3
E-MAIL ACCESS
Access, Login, Read, Delete, and/or Compose Email

Got A Surface Computer or a Handheld Device?

Touch the email icon to go to the email website. Enter your email ID and password. That's it—you are in. If you check the box to remember your login information, then accessing your email will be faster. Individuals in computer class have a new class email account. Other individuals have to register for a new account or use a previously set up email account.

Using A Senior Center or Library Computer
<u>With</u> a Desktop Email Icon?

Click the email icon to go to the email website. Enter your login information. That's it—you are in. On a public computer, you may not want to check the box to remember your login information.

Another Way to Log Into Your Yahoo Email Account
On Computers <u>Without</u> a Desktop Email Icon

Boot up. The Internet must be up to use email.

1. Click on the big alphabet e to open the Internet.

2. At the top of the screen, click in the URL box.

3. Backspace or press delete to erase what's in the box.

4. Key in yahoomail.com. Make the dot after the word mail with the period.

5. Wait for the login ID and password boxes to appear.

6. **Type your User Name ID correctly, no typos**. Here's an example: seniortechacademy@yahoo.com

7. Type in your password using the number keys at the top of the alphabet keys—no typos. Here's an example: 0010class.

8. Click on sign in.

9. Click on Keep Me Signed In (if it's your computer.)

10.   Click on the inbox to read your email.
11.   Click on New to write a new email.

Complete the Workshop 3 Hands-on Computer Practice. Access, Open, and Read Emails

1. Use a method such as the methods just described, to **access your email account**. There can be no typos in the ID or password. Check your class email address handout, first.

2. **Open and read your welcome emails**, especially the one from your computer class professor.

WORKSHOP 3
PROFESSIONALLY FORMAT E-MAIL
Compose and Send Email That Gets Read.

EMAIL ETIQUETTE AND SAFETY

- **Be nice**: Anything written and sent in an email should be OK for the entire world to hear about.

- **Avoid typing sentences in all caps**—this is like shouting.

- Always **key in a subject** pertaining to what your email is about.

- **Avoid keying emails when angry**.

- **Never discuss intimate details or gossip** and send it via email.

Complete Workshop 3 Hands-on Computer Practice 1.
Compose and Send Email

For this practice, send a hello or thank you email message to the senior center director. This is an example of a correctly formatted email.

Dear Senior Center Director
My main reason for taking this computer class is to learn how to sell our crafts online. Our closets are over flowing with homemade crafts.

I want to communicate with friends and family using email and social networks. I want to enjoy exploring the online world. Thanks for these Dr.Canty short, easy computer classes that make learning how to do these things possible.

Allen Aimsworth, Sr.
aimsworth007@yahoo.com

Complete Workshop 3 Hands-on Computer Practice 2.
Compose and send an email.

Step 1: View the example of a correctly formatted email.

Step 2: Access your email and click on the box with the word New or Compose.

Step 3: Key in the email address of the person the email will go to. **If there are typo's in an email address, the email will bounce back—not be sent**. The email address for the center director is in your class email address handout.

Step 4: Click on the line and key in a subject such as Hello from a Computer Class Student or Thank You From a Computer Academy Participant

Step 5: Key a greeting/salutation like: Hello, Good Morning, or just the individual's name like Dr. Canty. Press the enter key 1 or 2 times after keying the greeting.

Step 6: Key your message. A two or three sentence paragraph should do nicely.

Step 7: Press the enter key 2 times. Type your name.

Last Step: Press send.

WORKSHOP 3
OPEN AN EMAIL ATTACHMENT
Got A Paper Clip/Attachment Symbol
By the Email Message?

To open an **attachment**, click on the icon that looks like a paper clip. Some computers have software that checks the attachment to see if it is safe to open, or free of **viruses**. Some computer users open just the attachment(s) when they recognize the name of the sender, like emails and attachments from your professor. Photos and instructional documents are the most frequent email attachments in the senior center academy class emails.

Complete Workshop 3 Hands-on Computer Practice 3.
Open and Save An Email Attachment

1. Open the email from Professor Canty that has Class Photo in the subject line.

2. Click on the paper clip. Choose download attachment.

3. Save to your USB by clicking File, Save As.

4. Key the name my class photo.

5. Select the removable drive name to save it to.

6. Click Save.

Complete Workshop 1-3 Show & Tell Self-Test Part I
GETTING BETTER COMPUTER SKILLS/KNOWLEDGE, YET?

Answer correctly by writing in the requested information.

1. an example of a **URL** _____

2. an example of a valid **e-mail address** _____

3. list an **item on a Menu** _____

4. write what the symbol looks like to **Maximize** _____

5. write what the symbol looks like to **Minimize** _____

6. write what the **symbol** looks like to start the Internet from the
   Desktop _____

7. write the name of a **software package** we are learning to use in
   this class _____

8. write the name of a **piece of hardware** we use in the class
   _____

9. define **computer** _____

10.   define **technology**_____

11.   words keyed accurately per minute_____ with _____ errors

Complete Workshops 1-3 Show & Tell Self-Test Part II
Select the right answer by circling T, true or F, false.

1. Click on the icon with the big alphabet e to
open the Internet.   T   F

2. This is an example of an email **address**: yahoo.com.   T   F

3. This is an example of a **URL web address**:
 y@seniortechacademy. T   F

4. Entering the ID name and password is an example of
 logging in. T   F

5. Turning on the computer and waiting for it to bring up a screen is an
example of **logging in**.   T   F

6. In order to go to a **website address**, the Internet
 must be up. T   F

7. It's OK if a small error is made when **keying** a web or
email address. T   F

8. The **blinking, straight line** that shows up in a document or URL
box indicates that an error has been made. T   F

9. To click on, press the at sign key while holding down
the shift key. T   F

10.   To make the **@ symbol,** press the number 2 key while holding
down the shift key. T   F

11. An email or website address must be typed in all
capital letters. T   F

12. When goggling, a title, name, a topic must be entered
in the URL box. T   F

WORKSHOP 4
FACEBOOK SOCIAL NETWORK

USUALLY ANSWERS QUESTIONS SUCH AS
How can I show these spectacular event photos
to all my family and friends?

WORKSHOP 4
FACEBOOK SOCIAL NETWORK
Friend Me

One of the best things about **Facebook** is that you can see the past, present, and upcoming events **postings** of friends, family, communities or businesses. You can play games like Sudoku or Farmville, where your friends are your neighbors and you help each other out.

You can search for old friends from high school, old jobs, or just someone you lost contact with. Facebook has groups that you can join, and you get to select which groups, friends, and businesses you want to communicate with. Facebook is really big business. When you sign up as a fan of your favorite businesses, you will find coupons, giveaways, and great merchandise deals there for you, too.

Complete Workshop 4 Hands-on Computer Practice.

Go to **facebook.com**
1. Open a **Facebook account**.
2. Find family and/or friends.
3. Post a new photo and message to **your wall**.

Step 1. Click in the URL box.
Step 2. Type in facebook.com.
Step 3. Key the requested information in the fill in registration boxes. Your email address and password will be needed. Fill in your **Profile** information.
Step 4. Take a new photo or upload a photo stored on your USB.
Step 5. **Post** a new message such as a message about your participation in our computer academy workshop classes.
Step 6: Send and receive **friend requests.** You can send a friend request to this book's Facebook page. Choose to accept or not to accept **friends** requests. If you want to accept someone as a friend, **confirm** the friend request.

WORKSHOP 5   EBAY ONLINE SELLING

USUALLY ANSWERS QUESTIONS SUCH AS
Will people actually pay good money for this old thing?

One Man's Trash Is Another Man's Treasure
Turning Trash into Treasure on eBay

People who make crafts really like **etsy.com**. People who write books, or want to sell books like **amazon.com**. The largest marketplace in the world is **eBay**. Do you make crafts, have stuff from the old days, or have unused closet purchases that you want to get rid? Vast number of consumers frequent eBay in a single day, an estimated 70 to 100 million.

To reach these potential buyers, a seller's account or store have to be opened and a PayPal account. First, view a how to sell on eBay video at **youtube.com**.

eBay Selling How-Tos
How To Sell On eBay Step By Step Instructions

Practice—*just practice* **registering and setting up a seller's account, for technology learning purposes only**

www.ebay.com
STEP 1: Key in **www.ebay.com** and complete registration.

- Name your account based on the type of items that are going to be put up for sale.

- *A telephone number is required.* Go to your email to confirm.

www.paypal.com
STEP 2: Link your eBay account to **Paypal**. Do this in order to get paid or to buy. A bank account routing number and account number is required, or use a card. Suggestion: Use a bank other than a bank where your main money goes. In fact, it may be a good idea to set up a new checking account at a different bank just for eBay stuff.
Note: Both an eBay and a Paypal account have to be set up.

STEP 3: VERY, _VERY IMPORTANT_: Write down your user name and password, immediately, as soon as it is entered and accepted. **Email the user name and password to yourself for both accounts--the eBay account and for PayPal account.** If you do not enter the right user name and password, the accounts will not open.

Complete Workshop 5 hands-on Computer Practice.
List A Product On eBay.

- **Select a product to list bag** from bags 1-5.

- Practice--**List the product in your bag**. First, go to ebay.com. key in the name of the item in your bag to see if there are similar items like your item already listed? This will clue you in as to how to best list your item. Check during the 7 day auction period to see how bidding is going. Did your item sell?

WORKSHOP 6
WORD PROCESSING
CREATING DOCUMENTS

USUALLY ANSWERS QUESTIONS SUCH AS
Can you show me how to make a card and print it out?

Word Processing with Word

- **Flyer**
- **Greeting Card**
- **Newsletter article**
- **Calendar**
- **Letterhead**
- **Letter**
- **Business Cards**
- **Minutes of Meeting**
- **Manuscript**

"Let's make a flyer for our Saturday yard sale, Barb. Do you know how to use the new computer **Word software** to make the flyer, Kenny?" Let's not mess with the flyer thing right now. We really should be going out to Large Mart before the 5 o'clock traffic rush. We need a birthday card for our neighbor "like yesterday."

When Ken and Barbee learn how, they can make and print both the flyer and a birthday card in about 30 minutes or less. This will save time, money, and a rush hour traffic trip to the Large Mart. Would it benefit you to know how to use Word software to make and print some of your own useful documents? Which of the document listed in bold above, do you want to create and print during our workshop?

Workshop 6
WORD PROCESSING PREVIEW
Let's Navigate, Key & Design Text, Tweak & Print

Use Your Navigation Keys To Move About In a Document
To move around in a document, in addition to using a mouse, stylus, or touch screen, use keys with triangles, arrows, backspace, delete, redo, and undo.

Complete Workshop 6 Hands-on Computer Practice 1.
1. Make the @ at sign.
Practice this--Practice keying your email address.
Press and hold down the shift key and then press the number 2 key above the alphabet keys (hold down both the shift and number 2 key at the same time).

2. Make a **capital letter**.
Practice this: Practice capitalizing the first letter in your first and last name. First, press and hold down the shift key and then press the letter/alphabet that that you want capital. Press down both the shift key and the alphabet key to make a capital letter.

3. **Bold, italicize, underline**.

Practice this: Practice bolding, underlining, and italicizing your name. With Word open, look at the menu at the top and click the B. Start keying your name. This will bold everything as it is typed. Be sure to click the B again to stop bolding. The bold, italicize, and underline keys are toggles. To underline, **highlight** your name by clicking in front of it, then moving the mouse over it. The color will change which is highlighting. Look to the top of the screen. Click or press the I to italicize, and the U to underline. Click again to turn off italicize and underline.

4. **Make the dot in a URL website address**.

Practice this: Practice keying the URL address for yahoo.com. The period is used to make the dot in a Universal Resource Locator (URL) address. The period is on the 3rd row.

5. **Insert a clip art picture** or picture taken with a digital camera. **Practice this: Practice inserting a clip art picture of a computer; Next practice inserting your class photo from your USB.** With Word open, look at the top of the screen to the menus. Click on the word Insert then Picture. The picture for practice is your class photo—insert by clicking on from file, then USB removable drive. The second picture for practice is to click on Insert, clip art picture, look to the right, key in the word computer. Click on any computer picture to insert it.

6. Insert **Word Art**. Click on Insert, Picture, Word Art. When the word art screen appears type your name in 28 font, Script for practice.

Additional Workshop 6 Hands-on Computer Practice. Select and complete any 1 of 4.

1st Word Processing Lab   Create and Print a Greeting Card
Start by doing this:

1. Click on the Microsoft Office Word button located on the desktop.

2. Look to the top of the screen. Do you see a round circle with four different color squares? This is the **Office Button**.

3. Move the mouse arrow towards the top of the screen.

4. Point the arrow so that it is in the Office Button circle. Click on it.

5. After clicking the Office Button, another box of listings will appear.

6. Click on New. A listing of new documents will appear.

7. Scroll down to reach the word flyers.

8. Click on Flyers. Then events.

9. Click on Garage Sales. A new screen will appear with just the flyer.

10. Click on the word garage and a box will appear around it.

11. Delete the word garage, and press down caps lock key. Type the word yard so that it reads yard sale. Press the caps lock key again so that it will stop making all capital letters.

12. C lick in front of the date. Delete one letter at a time and replace it with the upcoming Saturday morning date. Change the start time to 8 and the ending time to 1.

13. Delete 1234 Elm and replace it with your first name so that it reads like this Richard Street.

2nd Word Processing Lab   Print A Document
1. **Print** a copy of your flyer by doing this: Look back up to the top of the screen. Click on the Office Button.

2. Scroll down to print. Move back up to find the picture of the printer. Click on it. Click in the circle that reads Print current page. Press OK.

3. Pick up your document from the printer.

3rd Word Processing Lab   Save A Word Document for Later Use
1. Move the mouse towards the top of the screen.

2. Point the arrow so that it is within the Office Button circle. Click on it.

3. Click on **SAVE AS**. When the other box opens, click on Word 97-2003 document.

4. When the other box appears, click on save in **My Documents**. Then name your document by typing in the File Name box the words yard sale flyer.

5. Then click in the **SAVE** box.

4th Word Processing Lab   Design & Print a Card

1.   Click on Office Button at the top of screen-- a circle and 4 colored boxes icon.

2.   When a drop down menu appears, click on New. A box saying new document will appear.

3.   Read down the list and stop at Greeting Cards. Click on it.

4.   When greeting cards open, Click on Occasions and special events. Scroll through until the birthday cards with balloons is located. It's in row 4, card three. Click on this card to download it. Wait.

5.   The card will open. Click on the box with Happy Birthday in it. Right Click to bring up a dialogue box that should have Edit Text. Type in someone's name or your name. Key something like Happy Birthday Don from Uncle Ben.

6.   Almost done. Click in the box with just one balloon. Type in a new, more personalized message—like enjoy and many more.

7.   Save the card to your USB flash drive. Print and/or email your birthday card.

WORKSHOP 7
POWERPOINT PRESENTATION

USUALLY ANSWERS QUESTIONS SUCH AS
Can you show me how to make my presentation more interesting?

POWERPOINT PRESENTATION PROJECT
Prepare Your 8-Slide PowerPoint Presentation

Speech, Presentation, & Photo Essay

These are the slide titles and completion instructions. Complete the **name slide, and choose 7 of the 9 remaining slide titles to complete**.

- Log into the PowerPoint presentation software like this.

Open Powerpoint software—To open PowerPoint, boot the system. When the desktop screen appears, find the big **P** icon and click on it. If you do not see a P icon on the desktop, click on Start, then Programs, Microsoft Office, then click on PowerPoint.

- Start preparing your presentation with the PowerPoint wizard.

Use the Powerpoint Wizard—look towards the top of the screen towards left and find the **Office button**—interlocking circles or squares.

- Select a **color, theme, layout design** for your presentation

by scrolling through the different themes and colors. Click on the different theme styles. Then select a theme of your choice.

- Use Insert **Clip Art** and a few words to on each slide.

- Save your presentation to your USB jump/flash drive.

- Present your **PowerPoint** to our class.

Slide 1 Name - Look to the top of the screen. Click Insert New Slide.

Slide 2 When I Grow Up
Click Insert New Slide.

Slide 3 Best Ever Place Visited
Click Insert New Slide.

Slide 4 Greatest Strength or Talent
Click Insert New Slide.

Slide 5 God Is or God Will
Click Insert New Slide.

Slide 6 Favorite Food
Click Insert New Slide.

Slide 7 Favorite Hobbies or Interests
Click Insert New Slide.

Slide 8 Something that You are Proud of Doing for yourself, for someone else.

Slide 9 A 3 or Less Words Description Of Yourself

Slide 10 Something that You Collect

1. Key your **full name** as the title for Slide 1. Insert **your photo** from your USB or take a photo.

2. Insert a clip art picture describing **something you always wanted to do or to be.** Type a few words about what you want to be when you grow up.

3. Insert a clip art picture and describe in a few words a **special location, vacation, spa, museum, church, ever visited**.

4. Insert a clip art picture and describe in a few words **what you know or others say that is your greatest strength or talent**.

5. Insert a clip art picture and describe in a few words **what God is or what God will do**.

6. Insert a clip art picture showing **your favorite food.** Type a few words about why this is your favorite food.

7. Insert a clip art picture describing **something you always wanted to do or to be.** Type a few words about what you want to be when you grow up.

8. Insert a clip art picture describing **something you are proud of?** Quit smoking, stopped cussing, lost weight, great check-up, etc.

9. What **1, 2, or 3 words best describes your life or personality**? Add clip art and the words.

WORKSHOP 8 BOOKS: CREATE & PUBLISH YOURS
USUALLY ANSWERS QUESTIONS SUCH AS
I want to write a book of poetry and a novel.
How can I do it without going broke, or spending more than $20.

Workshop 8
Hard Copy Handmade 10 Page Book
for Club, Class, Family or Other Local Distribution

Ken wants to write a children's short story book for their little grandson about his adventures as a long shore man. Barbee wants to pass on her top 10 man-pleasing recipes to their daughter-in-law. This workshop is exactly what is needed to show Barbee & Ken how to use their new computer to do this.

Complete this Workshop 8 Computer Lab Practice.
Make A Small Recipe Book with A Holiday Theme.

1. Get a sheet of light weight sheet of construction paper, 10 sheets of printer paper, and a stapler.

2. Open **Word**. Custom set the margins to 1 inch for the top margin and .5 inches for the other sides.

3. Decide on a short title or theme for your book. For this practice, let's use the title Valentine Day Recipes with a theme of 5 ingredient recipes. Key the title in font size 36. Key the theme in **font** size 24. Key the word by and your name in font size 18. Put the construction paper in the printer. Center the title, theme, and name information by looking to the top of the screen. Look for the second row with word paragraph. Click on the 2nd set of lines to center information. Print, then fold the sheet in half so that the title information appears on one half of the paper.

4. For this class workshop, we will make a class recipe book with each student contributing a recipe. Let's go to the Internet and search for a 5 ingredients or less recipe that appeals to your taste buds. Each participant is to contribute 1 recipe. Cut and past the Internet recipe you select to a Word document page. Modify and tweak the recipe to fit 1 page.

4. Be sure to include a reference notation as to whose recipe this is. After the recipe title, press Enter and key a new line like this as a reference: Mother Hubbard Cupboard Recipe Adapted and Modified by Computer Class Student Barbee.

5. Save your recipe file to your USB, then print a hard copy. A participant or the professor will collect each student's hard copy recipe. Open the folded construction sheet title page. Stack the recipe pages, then staple the pages to the inside top of the construction sheet cover page. Fold in half.

There it is—your hand made hard copy book.

Workshop 8
Createaspace Book Publishing Website
Hard Copy & Electronic E-Book Preparation To Sell on Amazon

Createaspace books must have at least 48 or more pages. Createaspacce provides the author with an ISBN book number and a copyright date. The rights to the book(s) are entirely all yours.

Complete this Workshop 8 Hands-on Computer Lab Practice. Create & Publish Your Own Book.

1. Go to **creaspace.com**

2. Create your account.

3. Decide on the size of the book.

4. Use the book margins specified by Createaspce to key the text in Word for your book. Upload your text file.

5. Create a cover page. Use a Createaspace cover and photos, or use your own photos.

6. Decide on pricing, marketing, and distribution channels like Amazon. Books are sold as hard copies and electronic copies.

7. Wait for the editors to proof your book—about 24 hours. You can order a proof hard copy, if you would like.

List your book on Amazon and other sites like Facebook. You are now a Createaspace published author.

WORKSHOP 9
HANDHELD COMPUTER DEVICES
How to Use More of the Features of an Ipad & Smartphone
USUALLY ANSWERS QUESTIONS SUCH AS
How do I send pictures from my cell?

WORKSHOP 9
HANDHELD DEVICES

More seniors are getting mobile, hand held devices like smartphones and iPads, especially as a gift from adult children. This workshop is an exploration into what hand held computer devices and their applications can do for seniors.

Take an **online virtual field trip** to hand held device vendor websites, how-to-video sites, and retail store sites.

Go on a **real time field trip** to a local hand held device retail shop that sells a lot of hand held devices.

Research at least one creative way to keep from losing a mobile device. Why? People use mobile devices for some serious stuff like a debit card to access money, a key to open and close cars, a home security monitoring device, a place to store documents like insurance cards, etc.

Think about it and **write down a suggestion for a useful app that is not yet on the market**? Hand held computer device screens seem to be getting smaller and smaller. Any suggestions out there to help people with low vision, or to accommodate customers who prefer larger screen mobile devices?

Workshop 9 Hands-on Handheld Computer Device Practice.

1. BYOD, Bring Your Own Device: Practice taking, sending, and posting photos with your own handheld device.

2. www.tech50plus.com: Go this website and find out what are the best products of the year for seniors in these categories: iPhones, smartwatches, tablets, portable computers, personal emergency response devices, point and shoot cameras, and automotive safety devices.

ABOUT THE AUTHOR

What Walt Disney did for some swamps of Orlando, Florida is similar to what Dr. Canty does for senior technology education. Dr. Canty is on a collaborative mission with senior centers, colleges, and universities to spread computer technology literacy among senior citizen populations in every county in North Carolina—county by county, 1 byte at a time.

To request a copy of the senior computer academy monthly newsletter, 1 Byte At A Time, email your name to Dr. Canty at seniortechacademy@yahoo.com.

THE END

New Technology Classes Continuously Forming

New classes start throughout the year. A new class usually starts each month. Computer classes are updated continuously and new workshop materials added as technology changes. Call the senior center director to let us know that you want to claim the computer lab seat and folder that will have your name it.

SOME SENIOR TECHNOLOGY ACADEMY
PARTICIPANT AFFLIATIONS

Apostolic Community Church PAW, Inc.
Bowens Chapel AME Zion Church
Brunswick County Senior Resource Center
Cape Fear Baptist Church
Cape Fear Community College Continuing Ed.
Columbus County Senior Center, Ransom
Creekwood Housing Education Center
Disabled American Veterans (DAV)
East Columbus Senior Center
Ebenezer Missionary Baptist Church
First Baptist Missionary Church
First Born Holiness Church
Gregory Congregational Church
Johnson Chapel AMEZ Church
Hillcrest Housing Education Center
Leland Senior Center
Lighthouse Shining Ministries
Leon Mann Enrichment Center
Macedonia Fire Baptized Church
Macedonia Missionary Baptist Church
Moore's Chapel Missionary Baptist
Mt. Calvary Missionary Baptist Church
Mt. Nebo Baptist Church
Mt. Olive AME Church
Mt. Pilgrim Missionary Baptist Church
New Hanover County Senior Center
Prayer and Bible Church
Progressive Lodge #830
Shiloh Missionary Baptist Church
Shining Light Ministries
St. Andrews AME Zion Church
St. Luke AME Zion Church
St. Stephens AME Church
Summerville AMEZ Church
Union Missionary Baptist Church
United Senior Citizens Club
United States Air Force
United States Army
United States Civil Service
United States Marine Corps
United States Navy
University of North Carolina Wilmington OLLI
Veterans Foreign Wars (VFW)
Walter's Chapel AME Zion Church
Williston Alumni Class '62

www.ingramcontent.com/pod-product-compliance
Lightning Source LLC
Chambersburg PA
CBHW060504060326
40689CB00020B/4630